Think Before You Run

By

Felicia Robertson

Copyright © 2024 **Felicia Robertson**

All Rights Reserved

ISBN:

Dedication

In the creation of "Think Before You Run," a book that delves into the poignant themes of runaways and the specter of death, we owe our deepest gratitude to those who have supported us on this challenging yet enlightening journey:

To the runaway youth whose stories of resilience, struggles, and pain have inspired this work, we offer our utmost respect and admiration. Your courage in the face of adversity has left an indelible mark on us.

To those who have lost loved ones to the unforgiving hands of fate, we extend our sincerest condolences. Your strength and the memories of those who have departed too soon have shaped the profound reflections within these pages.

To our families, friends, and loved ones, whose unwavering love, patience, and understanding have sustained us through the tumultuous process of creation, we offer our heartfelt thanks. Your support has been our guiding light.

To the professionals, experts, and advocates in the fields of mental health, social work, and crisis intervention who tirelessly work to support and protect vulnerable individuals, we acknowledge your invaluable contributions to our understanding of these critical issues.

To the editorial team at *Amazon KDP Publishers*, whose dedication and keen insights have helped us refine our words and ideas, we are grateful for your expertise and guidance.

To the readers who now hold this book in their hands, we humbly offer our work as insights have helped us refine our words and ideas. We are grateful for your expertise and guidance.

To the readers who now hold this book in their hands, we humbly offer our work as a reflection of the human experience-its joys, its sorrows, and the profound lessons that come from contemplating our mortality.

May "Think Before You Run" serve as a reminder to cherish every moment, to seek understanding and empathy, and to embrace life with courage and compassion.

With heartfelt gratitude and introspection,

Felicia Robertson

Acknowledgment

In loving memory of my dear daughter, a runaway free spirit,
Whose laughter and courage forever in my heart will lift.
Though your journey led you far from home's embrace,
Your spirit roams free in a timeless, boundless space.
With each step you took on paths unknown and wide,
You showed the world a fire that never died.
Through valleys dark and mountains steep you'd roam,
A wild and fearless soul far away from home.
Your absence leaves a void that none can fill,
Yet in memories, you live vivid and still.
Your light shines bright in every starlit night,
Guiding me through shadows, a beacon of light.
Though you left this world too soon, my runaway child,
Your spirit lives on in the wind, free and wild.
In the tapestry of my life, you'll always be,
A cherished memory, forever roaming free.
Rest in peace, my dear daughter, in fields of gold,
Where runaway dreams and stories untold,
Live on in eternity's endless embrace,
A legacy of love and courage, your grace.

About the Author

Felicia Robertson who overcame the loss of her daughter but has created a safe space for other Runaway's and victims of human trafficking

"In the depths of my grief, I found purpose. Through the pain of loss, I discovered strength. Today, I stand not as a victim of tragedy but as a beacon of hope for those who seek refuge and healing. Together, we rewrite our stories, reclaim our voices, and build a sanctuary where broken wings learn to soar again.".

Felicia Robertson

In the bustling world of culinary arts, advocacy, and literature, there exists a remarkable individual who seamlessly weaves through diverse roles with grace and determination. Meet Felicia Robertson, a visionary Director of Culinary, Mandated Reporter, loving Mother, and passionate College Graduate. With a pen as mighty as a chef's knife, Felicia Robertson is not only the mastermind behind the insightful book *"Think Before You Run,"* but also the author of the empowering *"Bismillah: With Growth and Development Comes Change."*

Beyond the kitchen and the written word, Felicia Robertson stands as a staunch advocate for runaways, lending her voice to the voiceless and fighting against the heinous crime of human trafficking. Her tireless efforts and unwavering commitment to these causes have earned her the title of a warrior in the battle for justice and compassion.

A beacon of inspiration and change, Felicia Robertson exemplifies the power of empathy, education, and action. Through her work and dedication, she not only nourishes bodies with culinary delights but also nurtures minds and spirits with wisdom and courage. In a world filled with challenges and adversity, Felicia Robertson shines brightly as a beacon of hope, resilience, and positive transformation.

CONTENTS

Dedication i

Acknowledgment iii

About the Author iv

Preface 1

Introduction 3

Chapter 1 She Was Born 13

Chapter 2 Shining Personality 22

Chapter 3 She Was a Bright Student 31

Chapter 4 She Missed the Path 44

Chapter 5 A Light Gone Too Soon 50

Chapter 6 Deceit 57

Chapter 7 Footprints in the sand 62

Closing Thoughts 64

Preface

In the shadows of our society, there exists a silent epidemic that preys on the vulnerable and the lost. It is a tale as old as time, yet it continues to haunt us with its devastating consequences. This is the story of a runaway child whose journey of escape and rebellion led to a tragic end, one that serves as a stark reminder of the dangers that lurk in the darkness.

As we venture into the pages of this book, we are confronted with the harsh realities faced by countless youths who find themselves adrift in a world that offers little solace or guidance. Through the eyes of our protagonist, we witness the tumultuous path of a young soul seeking refuge from a troubled past, only to stumble upon a dangerous escape route that leads to a fateful decision.

The story of this runaway child serves as a poignant narrative of the perils of addiction, of the consequences of wrong choices made in moments of desperation and despair. It is a tale that compels us to reflect on the fragility of life, the power of resilience, and the importance of reaching out to those in need before it is too late.

As you immerse yourself in the unfolding tragedy of this young runaway, may you be moved to empathy, compassion, and action. Let us not forget that behind every statistic, every headline, there lies a human soul yearning for understanding, for redemption, for a second chance.

Through the pages of this book, may we honor the memory of those who have succumbed to the darkness, and may we strive to shine a light of hope and healing for those who still wander lost and join us on this journey of reflection.

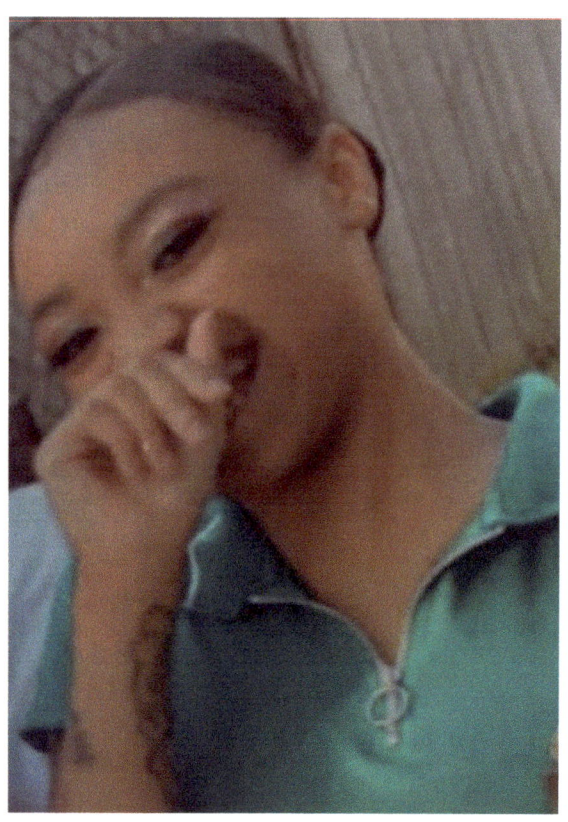

Al-Baqarah - 2:286

Allah does not require of any soul more than what it can afford. All good will be for its own benefit, and all evil will be to its own loss. "The believers pray," "Our Lord! Do not punish us if we forget or make a mistake. Our Lord! Do not place a burden on us like the one you placed on those before us. Our Lord! Do not burden us with what we cannot bear. Pardon us, forgive us, and have mercy on us. You are our "only' Guardian.

So, grant us victory over the disbelieving people."

Introduction

As I took my first breath in this world, I was born into a sea of tears. They were my mother's tears flowing freely down her cheeks, a testament to the immense pain and uncertainty that engulfed her. At that very moment, she had just been handed a sentence—a ten-year and eleven-month federal sentence that would separate us for what felt like an eternity.

Fear gripped her heart as she questioned her ability to protect me throughout the long and arduous journey ahead. How would she shield me from the world's harsh realities for the next seven years and nine months? It was a daunting prospect, but she clung to her strong faith in Allah (God), knowing that He had guided her through trials in the past and would do so again.

My mother's devotion to her faith was not just a source of comfort for her but also a guiding light for me. It was through her example that I learned the true power of faith and the importance of putting our trust in something greater than ourselves. She inspired me to stay strong during tough times.

As she prayed, I could see the peacefulness that washed over her, and it was contagious. I, too, found myself feeling more centered and grounded in the presence of her faith. Her prayers were a reminder that we are never truly alone and that there is always someone watching over us, guiding us, and protecting us.

Even though she was physically absent, her faith was a constant presence in my life. It gave me hope, strength, and a sense of purpose. I will forever be grateful to my mother for showing me the transformative power of faith and for instilling in me a deep sense of trust in Allah.

I was blessed to have guardians, my aunts Debra and Dakota and my uncle Bobby. Little did I know then that my cousins would play a significant role in shaping my upbringing. Although I was not yet aware of the profound impact they would have on my life, the love and care they provided were a testament to the influence of my Ummi (mother). Even in her absence, her love radiated through them, guiding me on the path of love and resilience.

By the way, my name is Starte Leoniece Grace Thomas. However, I was known by various names throughout my life—Star, Lady Mayweather, Queen Bee, Starte Ballin Thomas, and Starte Robertson. These were my Facebook celebrity names, remnants of a digital presence my mother couldn't bear to erase. Her heartache was too profound to silence the voice I once had in the world.

At the young age of thirteen, I kicked off my runaway adventures, fueled by an eagerness to experience the supposed excitement and thrill that the world had to offer. I couldn't bear the thought of missing out on all the fun. Playing a constant game of cat and mouse with my mom added an element of excitement to my escapades. I reveled in the chase, unaware of the pain and hardships my actions inflicted upon others. It didn't cross my mind how much my decisions would burden my loved ones.

I used the Children Family Services as a weapon, a way to make my voice heard and ensure my perspective was taken seriously. Looking back, I wish I could rewrite my story with different choices. But now, as I rest in peace, all I can do is hope that my struggles serve as a cautionary tale, guiding you to live a life that fulfills the dreams I left unfinished.

My grandmother instilled in my mom the value of obedience, but their relationship remained strained, making it difficult for me to comprehend how my life might have turned out differently if those lessons had been consistently applied.

> *"Listen, my son, to your father's instruction and do not forsake your mother's teaching. They will be a garland to grace your head and a chain to adorn your neck."*
>
> *Proverbs 1:8-9*
>
> *"He who obeys instructions guards' life, but he who is contemptuous of his ways will die,"*
>
> *Proverbs 19:16*

The Bible, too, emphasizes the importance of obeying our parents and cherishing their teachings. But what happens when those elders and parents become the source of harm, crossing boundaries and causing pain? It's a tough question to grapple with, especially when the very people who should protect us are the ones causing harm.

Another pressing issue arises: How do you find the courage to speak up when you face violations at school, in your own home, or even at a friend's place? In the midst of such adversity, it's crucial to seek help and trust someone. Reach out by dialing a helpline, confiding in a school counselor, seeking refuge in a local place of worship, or turning to a trusted aunt or uncle. And if those options fail, confide in a loyal friend. You should never bear the weight of your pain alone. Remember, God is with you, and He wants the best for your life. Don't let the predators steal your joy. Protect your happiness and think carefully before making any rash decisions. Refuse to be forced into dangerous situations.

At the age of eighteen, I found myself in a dusty, cold, and empty room in Chicago—a room that would become my final resting place. I overdosed a victim of circumstances and a world that had failed to protect me. The ghost of my memory haunts my mother's thoughts day in and day out, an eternal reminder of the profound loss she endured.

But even in death, my journey did not end. I became a photographer in training, capturing the world through a different lens. Time, however, showed no patience for beginners, and my journey was cut short far too soon. As a believer in Islam, I understood the concept of Qadr—the divine decree that shows Allah's omniscience and unlimited power. Everyone, at some point in their life, must answer to Allah. I had not planned to meet my Qadr so soon, but it was a reminder that our destinies were in the hands of a higher power.

I was introduced to Islam by my mother. We identified with each other as I was intrigued by her head covering. I wanted to wear it for a while. As I grew older, she was struggling to hold her beliefs together, so I found an escape for myself, and eventually, I quit wearing my Hijab. I always identified as a Muslima. I just wanted to see life from other angles to be sure of what it was I believed in. The devil can trick even the best of us.

On the Day of my funeral, my mommy's words to me were;

Dear Star,

My world revolved around protecting my baby girl. I named you Star because you were the light of my life in my darkest hours. My children meant that God Had shown me his Mercy, Love, and plans for my life. You are loved and will always be the heartbeat in my life with a heightened beat. There was never a dull moment for us. You kept me on my toes and in commune with God. My twin in every way. We were too much alike.

Forever and always,

Love Mommy.

Allah knew my Mommy was heartbroken and shattered, so he sent Mrs. Lorna M. Pettis to answer her for me. When tomorrow starts without me, And I am not here to see If the sun should rise and find your eyes, filled with tears for me.

I wish so much you would not cry the way you did today while thinking of the many things we did not get to say. I know how much you love me, as much as I love you, and each time you think of me, I know you will miss me too. When tomorrow starts without me, do not think we are far apart, for every time you think of me, I am right there in your heart.

My death had drained the essence from my mother, which breaks my heart into a million pieces. She just kept trying to see if she had done things differently and what the outcome would have been. When I overdosed on the world, I captured it through my camera lenses when I was at Northwest Passage. The only way I live the dream is if I can live it through you. Please think before you run. If you are unsafe at home, then report it. No one should have to live with the dysfunction of someone else. Life is already hard.

Remember, you are a beautiful woman and handsome man perfectly created by Allah SWT (God). Believe in yourself and the power you have. You cannot let your voice be silent. Be bold. See something, say something. Every year, young men and women are trafficked all over the world. They trick us into believing they want to help us find our way in the industry.

I rapped and danced. I was brainwashed into believing he loved me, and we were building together. Instead, he was exploiting my youth and my beauty. I wish I could see through this earlier. He was hoping that I would recruit more young women. I would not have known any better. God has protected me from further abuse. I left on an earlier flight to eternity.

Trust is crucial, but for a wrong person, it can be brutal. He left some words that I am sharing with you today in *Think Before You Run*. Inside this book are the photos of Life that Allah SWT has allowed me to share with you after my death. I took these photos at seventeen.

What if I could have lived longer? The possibilities of life would have been endless.

Now, I have joined my cousin Chartez and my cousin Von in the afterlife. Charter was twenty-one years old when he passed, and Von was eighteen like me. Someone cut our lives short. We had a future planned. A future we will never be allowed to love. Live for us. You have the power to change the world.

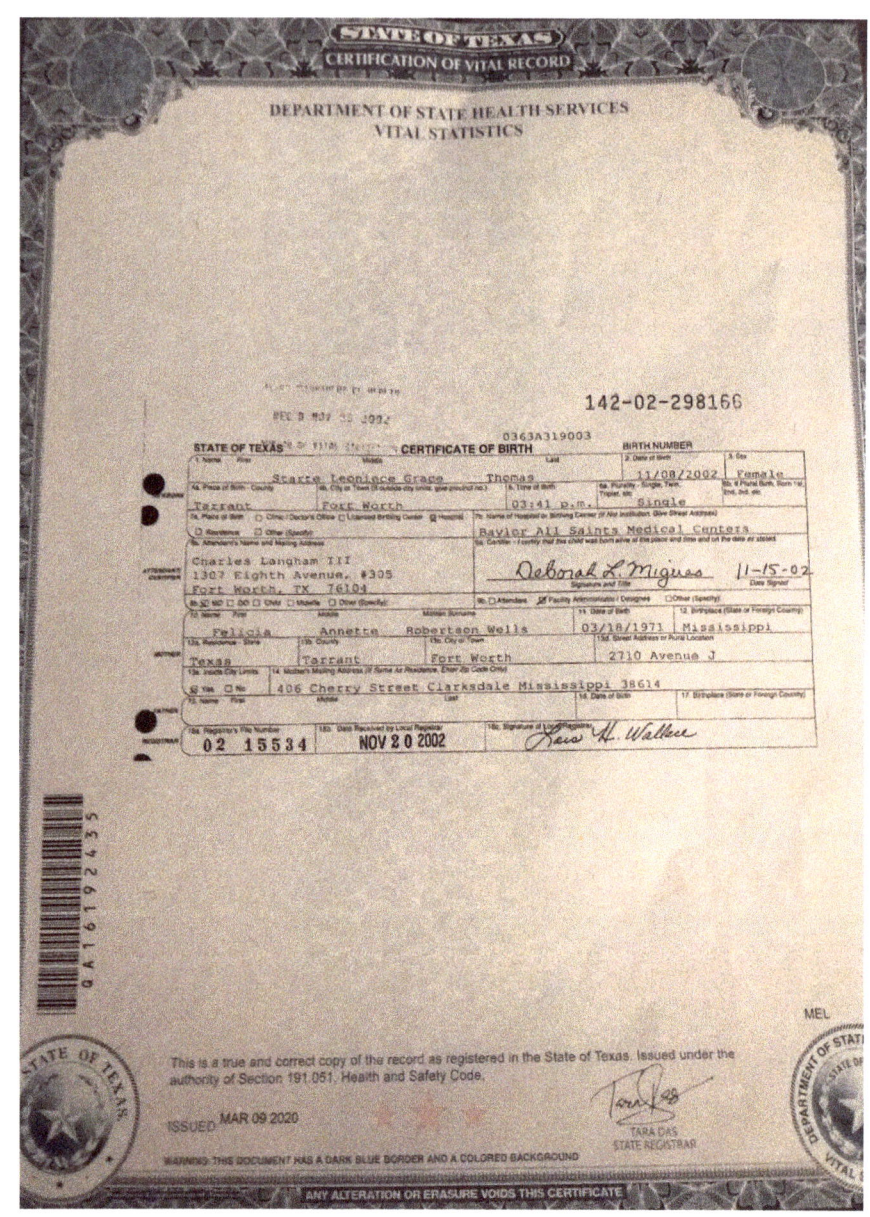

Chapter 1
She Was Born

Life can be unpredictable and full of unexpected challenges. Despite my best efforts, my journey with my daughter Starte was no exception. Her arrival into this world was met with unforeseen hardships, and circumstances beyond my control threatened to tear us apart. The pain of being separated from my daughter was immeasurable, and I found myself grappling with heartbreak and longing. Yet, even in the darkest of times, my love for Starte remained unyielding, a flame that burned brightly and kept me going.

"And We have enjoined upon man [care] for his parents. His mother carried him, [increasing her] in weakness upon weakness, and his weaning is in two years. Be grateful to Me and your parents; to Me is the [final] destination."

- (Quran 31:14)

This verse constantly reminds us of the profound beauty of motherhood. It acknowledges the physical and emotional struggles that I, as a mother, have experienced while carrying and nurturing my child. It also emphasizes the importance of expressing gratitude to Allah and my parents for the gift of life and the opportunity to embark on this incredible journey of motherhood. Through the ups and downs, the love and devotion that I pour into raising my child reflect the immeasurable beauty that lies within being a mother.

In the depths of my soul, there exists a story. A story intertwined with love, loss, and an unbreakable bond that transcends all boundaries. It is a story that has shaped me, touched me, and left an indelible mark on my heart.

When I think back to the day I discovered that tiny life was blossoming within me, my heart swelled with a mix of emotions. Joy, excitement, and a hint of trepidation coursed through my veins. It was a moment of profound realization that life was about to change in the most beautiful and unpredictable ways. As I nurtured the precious secret growing within, I envisioned a future filled with laughter, dreams, and endless love.

"And We have enjoined upon man [care] for his parents. His mother carried him, [increasing her] in weakness upon weakness, and his weaning is in two years. Be grateful to Me and your parents; to Me is the [final] destination."

-   (Quran 31:14)

Most of the time, I end up thinking deeply about how the Holy Quran is like a life map for us. It has everything we need to know about the miracles around us.

The months that followed were a roller coaster of emotions. I marveled at the miracle taking place within my body, feeling the fluttering kicks that connected me to a soul yet to be born.

Each day, I watched with awe as my belly swelled. My heart would just skip a beat. As the days turned into weeks and the weeks into months, I watched in awe as my body blossomed.

With each passing day, my connection to the growing life intensified. I reveled in the mysterious dance of flutters and kicks, marveling at the miracle unfolding within me. I imagined the little one's delicate features, the curve of their tiny fingers, and wondered whether they would inherit my eyes or their father's smile.

The anticipation of discovering the baby's gender was palpable. It was as though the secret held within my womb held the key to unlocking a world of dreams and possibilities. I delighted in the mystery, imagining a future filled with laughter and adventures, whether it be a daughter to share secrets and tea parties with or a son to teach the wonders of the world.

But beyond the curiosity of gender, there was a deeper transformation occurring within me. My perspective on life shifted as though a veil had been lifted, revealing the profound interconnectedness of all things. I found myself cherishing the simplest of moments—a gentle breeze caressing my skin, the sound of birdsong on a crisp morning, the tender touch of a loved one's hand—knowing that soon, I would share these wonders with my child.

During pregnancy, my body changed, and so did my heart. A love like no other began to arise within me, fierce and unyielding. I would cradle my growing belly with tenderness, whispering words of love and promises of protection. I could feel the weight of responsibility settling upon my shoulders, and I embraced it willingly, knowing that I was embarking on the most sacred of journeys.

Just as my pregnancy progressed, I experienced a hurricane of emotions. From the awe-inspiring feeling of life growing within me to the occasional moments of uncertainty and fear, I crossed the beautiful complexities of carrying a child. Each day brought me closer to holding my precious baby in my arms, and my love for her blossomed with every passing moment. I had many plans for her like any other mother would do for her child.

> *"Whoever saves one [a life], it is as if he had saved mankind entirely."*
>
> *- (Quran 5:32)*

As I reflect on the importance of life, this verse resonates deeply within me. It reminds me that every life is precious and holds immense value. The birth of my child is a testament to the miracle of life itself, and I am entrusted with the responsibility to protect and nurture this precious gift.

Each day, I strive to create a loving and nurturing environment for my child, knowing that by doing so, I am contributing to the well-being and preservation of humanity as a whole. This verse reinforces the profound impact that even a single life can have, and it fills my heart with a sense of purpose and gratitude.

*****

Coming back to the moment of her birth, precisely nine months after her conception, Starte entered this world and was welcomed into my waiting arms. The rush of emotions that surged through me in that instant is something I can never forget. As I held her delicate form against my chest, a profound mixture of awe, joy, and overwhelming love engulfed my entire being.

Gazing into her innocent eyes, I was struck by the sheer miracle of life unfolding before me. Her tiny fingers curled around mine as if seeking reassurance and connection in this vast and unfamiliar world. The weight of responsibility settled upon my shoulders, mingling with an indescribable tenderness that astounded me.

In that sacred moment, time seemed to stand still. Every worry, every fear, every hardship I had ever faced faded into insignificance, eclipsed by the radiant presence of this precious soul cradled in my arms. It was as if the universe had conspired to present me with the greatest treasure, an embodiment of hope and endless possibilities.

The softness of her delicate skin, the faint scent of new life, and the gentle rise and fall of her chest as she took her first breaths—all these sensory details etched themselves deeply into my memory. I marveled at the perfection of her tiny features, marveling at the miraculous intricacies that had formed within her. Her every movement, every sound, became a symphony that resonated within the depths of my soul.

Overwhelmed by a surge of maternal instinct, I vowed to protect her, nurture her, and guide her through the labyrinth of life that lay ahead. I knew that my love for her would be unwavering, serving as a fortress against the trials and tribulations she would inevitably encounter. At that moment, I made a silent promise to be her shelter, her guiding light, and her ultimate source of support.

As I held Starte in my arms, the world around me faded into the background, and it was just the two of us, connected by an unbreakable bond. It was in that embrace that I realized the immense power of a mother's love—a love that transcends words, that defies all logic and surges with an intensity that cannot be contained.

In the depths of my heart, I knew that this precious being cradled in my arms would forever be the embodiment of my hopes, dreams, and aspirations. Every beat of my heart, every breath I took, would now be dedicated to her well-being and happiness. The first glimpse in her eyes, I gazed into her innocent eyes. I whispered a silent prayer, fervently hoping that I would be worthy of the tremendous privilege bestowed upon me—being her mother.

The birth of my little one, although seemingly simple and joyful, was anything but ordinary. You see, at the time of her arrival, I was serving a federal sentence and found myself confined within the walls of a correctional facility. The circumstances surrounding her birth were not typical, and I was faced with the harsh realities and emotional turmoil of life behind bars.

The weight of my situation was overwhelming, and I had to navigate complex challenges while dealing with the daily struggles of prison life. Despite all of this, the birth of my child brought a glimmer of hope and joy into my life, reminding me that even in the darkest of places, there is still beauty and love to be found.

"And We have certainly honored the children of Adam and carried them on land and sea and provided for them of the good things and preferred them over much of what We have created, with [definite] preference."

- (Quran 17:70)

This verse reminds me of the inherent honor and dignity that is bestowed upon every human being, including my child and myself. It acknowledges that Allah has entrusted us with a unique purpose and has blessed us with the ability to navigate the world and experience the bounties of life.

Being a mother, I am humbled by the responsibility to nurture and guide my children, knowing that they are part of this honorable lineage of the children of Adam. This verse reinforces the immense value and significance of life and encourages me to cherish and protect it, celebrating the beauty of existence itself.

In my journey as a mother, these verses from the Quran serve as constant reminders of the beauty and sanctity of motherhood, as well as the importance of safeguarding the gift of life. They inspire me to continue nurturing and cherishing my child, knowing that each moment is a precious opportunity to fulfill the profound responsibilities and joys that come with being a mother.

Chapter 2
Shining Personality

Starte Leoniece Grace Thomas was not just a name; it was a tapestry of identities woven through the experiences and influences of her childhood. My daughter had amazing people to look at when growing up beside me. Her guardians, her Aunts Debra and Dakota and Uncle Bobby played pivotal roles in shaping the person she was. Each guardian brought a unique perspective to her upbringing, creating a rich environment where she thrived.

Debra, the eldest one, was a nurturing presence, always emphasizing the importance of education and discipline. Her influence instilled in Starte a love for learning and a sense of responsibility. Debra would often sit with Starte, helping her with schoolwork and encouraging her to ask questions and seek knowledge. She introduced Starte to the world of books, opening her eyes to different cultures, ideas, and histories. Debra's love for reading was infectious, and soon, Starte found herself lost in the pages of novels, traveling to far-off lands and experiencing lives different from her own.

Dakota, on the other hand, was the free spirit, encouraging Starte to explore her creativity and embrace her vibrant personality. Dakota believed in the power of self-expression and often organized art projects and creative activities at home. She introduced Starte to music, dance, and painting, allowing her to experiment with different forms of art. Dakota's influence helped Starte develop a keen sense of aesthetics and an appreciation for the beauty in everyday life. It was Dakota who gave Starte her first camera, a simple point-and-shoot, but it was enough to spark a lifelong passion.

Uncle Bobby, with his quiet strength, taught her the value of resilience and the importance of standing up for oneself. Bobby was a man of few words, but his actions spoke volumes. He would take Starte on long walks, sharing stories of his own life and the challenges he had overcome. Through these stories, Starte learned about perseverance, courage, and the importance of staying true to oneself. Bobby's presence was a comforting constant in her life, a reminder that no matter what happened, she was never alone.

My daughter was a beautiful young lady with so many different aspects to her personality. She was a wonderful puzzle of emotions, a combination of smart yet kind, sweet, and humble. She had a real passion for things. I could see it in her eyes.

Maybe it was because of her multifaceted personality that she had so many different names. Each name was a reflection of the different aspects of her identity. "Star Lady Mayweather" spoke to her fierce independence and ability to defend herself when necessary, a nod to her inner strength and resilience. "Queen Bee Starte Ballin Thomas" captured her vibrant, larger-than-life personality, one that could light up any room she walked into. "Starte Robertson," her Facebook celebrity name, symbolized her digital presence and the voice I couldn't bear to silence, even in her absence.

Amidst these identities, Starte discovered a profound passion for photography. This love for capturing moments started at a young age, nurtured by Dakota's encouragement to see the world through a different lens. Photography became more than just a hobby; it was a way for Starte to express herself and make sense of the world around her. Each click of the shutter was a glimpse into her soul, revealing her unique perspective and her deep connection to the beauty and pain of life.

With her camera in hand, Starte roamed the streets, capturing the essence of her surroundings. Her photographs told stories of joy, sorrow, resilience, and hope. She had an uncanny ability to find beauty in the mundane, turning everyday moments into extraordinary works of art. Her unique perspective allowed her to see the world in ways others couldn't, and she used her photography to share that vision with the world.

Starte's favorite subjects were the people around her. She loved capturing candid moments, the raw emotions that people often tried to hide. Her photos of street vendors, children playing, and elderly couples walking hand in hand were more than just images; they were narratives of life, each telling a unique story. Other than those, she loved nature. She used to love capturing all these different kinds of flowers, and she loved to capture the inner beauty that others could not see. Her pictures of flowers, leaves, or just nature overall are amazing to look at. I still have them and when I look at them, I realize how talented my daughter was.

Her photos of Aunt Debra lost in a book, Dakota dancing in the living room, and Uncle Bobby sitting silently on the porch were some of her most treasured pieces, each capturing the essence of her guardians and the love they had given her.

Despite the challenges and hardships she faced, Starte's guardians ensured that her upbringing was filled with love and support. They created a haven where she could explore her passions and develop her talents. This foundation of love and stability was crucial in helping Starte navigate the complexities of life, providing her with the strength to overcome the obstacles that lay ahead.

sorrow, resilience, and hope. She had an uncanny ability to find beauty in the mundane, turning everyday moments into extraordinary works of art. Her unique perspective allowed her to see the world in ways others couldn't, and she used her photography to share that vision with the world.

Starte's favorite subjects were the people around her. She loved capturing candid moments, the raw emotions that people often tried to hide. Her photos of street vendors, children playing, and elderly couples walking hand in hand were more than just images; they were narratives of life, each telling a unique story. Other than those, she loved nature. She used to love capturing all these different kinds of flowers, and she loved to capture the inner beauty that others could not see. Her pictures of flowers, leaves, or just nature overall are amazing to look at. I still have them and when I look at them, I realize how talented my daughter was.

Her photos of Aunt Debra lost in a book, Dakota dancing in the living room, and Uncle Bobby sitting silently on the porch were some of her most treasured pieces, each capturing the essence of her guardians and the love they had given her.

Despite the challenges and hardships she faced, Starte's guardians ensured that her upbringing was filled with love and support. They created a haven where she could explore her passions and develop her talents. This foundation of love and stability was crucial in helping Starte navigate the complexities of life, providing her with the strength to overcome the obstacles that lay ahead.

As she grew older, Starte's love for photography deepened, becoming an integral part of her identity. It was through her lens that she found solace and purpose, a way to process her emotions and connect with others. Her photographs became a testament to her journey, capturing not just the world around her but the essence of who she was.

In these formative years, Starte's guardians imparted lessons that would stay with her for a lifetime. Debra's emphasis on education, Dakota's encouragement of creativity, and Bobby's quiet strength all played a part in shaping the woman Starte would become. They taught her to be resilient, to embrace her individuality, and to find beauty in the world, no matter how difficult life became.

Her journey as a photographer was just beginning. She dreamed of traveling the world, capturing the diverse cultures, landscapes, and faces that populated the globe. Her camera was not just a tool but an extension of her soul, allowing her to share her perspective and connect with people from all walks of life. Each photograph was a piece of her heart, a glimpse into the world as she saw it—a world filled with beauty, pain, joy, and resilience.

Chapter 3
She Was a Bright Student

At the core of her being, Star Lady Mayweather was a nomad, a seeker of adventure and knowledge. Born Starte Leoniece Grace Thomas, she had been known by many names throughout her life, each one representing a different phase of her journey. From Queen Bee Starte Ballin Thomas to simply Starte Robertson, she embraced each identity with the same restless spirit and insatiable curiosity.

It was at the tender age of thirteen that Starte's wanderlust first ignited. Fueled by a desire to break free from the confines of her small-town upbringing, she embarked on her first runaway adventure. Her mind was consumed with visions of exotic lands and far-off cities, eager to experience all the wonders the world had to offer.

Raised in a loving and supportive household, Starte's urge to wander seemed somewhat out of place. Her Aunt Debra, Dakota, and Uncle Bobby had provided her with a nurturing environment, encouraging her interests and fostering her growth. But despite this stable foundation, there was always a pull towards the unknown for Starte. A yearning deep within her soul to discover what lay beyond the safety of home.

And so, she ran. Each escape was a thrilling gamble, a mix of fear and exhilaration as she navigated the streets as a young girl alone in the world. It was here that she encountered people from all walks of life - some kind and helpful, others dangerous and untrustworthy. Through these interactions, she learned valuable lessons about both the harshness and beauty of humanity.

For Starte, running away was not just about physical movement but also about pushing herself to new limits. Each time she set foot on those unfamiliar streets, she challenged herself to be brave and resilient in the face of unknown dangers. And though her escapades were often riddled with peril, they also brought moments of pure wonder and excitement that fueled her thirst for adventure even more.

Starte's wild and rebellious spirit often led her down paths of adventure, but not without consequence. Her frequent runaways became a constant game of cat and mouse with her mother, each time resulting in a complex mix of emotions. Starte's mother, desperate to keep her daughter safe, would tirelessly search for her every time she disappeared. But for Starte, these escapes were a form of rebellion, a way to assert her independence and explore the world on her terms.

This constant tension between mother and daughter gave way to moments of conflict and misunderstanding. Though deeply concerned for her daughter's safety, Starte's mother could not understand her need for freedom and exploration. And for Starte, these runaways only fueled her desire to break free from the suffocating expectations placed upon her.

The emotional toll on both mother and daughter was immense, shaping their relationship in profound ways. Each time Starte returned home, the air was thick with unspoken words and simmering tensions. Her mother's relief was always overshadowed by a lingering fear of the next time Starte might vanish. This strained relationship was marked by a push and pull, with Starte constantly testing the limits of her freedom while her mother grappled with the anxiety and helplessness of potentially losing her daughter for good.

The cycle of leaving and returning created an intricate emotional labyrinth that they navigated together, with each journey leaving deeper imprints on their hearts. And though they may struggle to understand each other's perspectives at times, their love for one another remains steadfast in the face of their turbulent dynamic.

Starte's wild and rebellious spirit often led her down paths of adventure, but not without consequence. Her frequent runaways became a constant game of cat and mouse with her mother, each time resulting in a complex mix of emotions. Starte's mother, desperate to keep her daughter safe, would tirelessly search for her every time she disappeared. But for Starte, these escapes were a form of rebellion, a way to assert her independence and explore the world on her terms.

This constant tension between mother and daughter gave way to moments of conflict and misunderstanding. Though deeply concerned for her daughter's safety, Starte's mother could not understand her need for freedom and exploration. And for Starte, these runaways only fueled her desire to break free from the suffocating expectations placed upon her.

The emotional toll on both mother and daughter was immense, shaping their relationship in profound ways. Each time Starte returned home, the air was thick with unspoken words and simmering tensions. Her mother's relief was always overshadowed by a lingering fear of the next time Starte might vanish. This strained relationship was marked by a push and pull, with Starte constantly testing the limits of her freedom while her mother grappled with the anxiety and helplessness of potentially losing her daughter for good.

The cycle of leaving and returning created an intricate emotional labyrinth that they navigated together, with each journey leaving deeper imprints on their hearts. And though they may struggle to understand each other's perspectives at times, their love for one another remains steadfast in the face of their turbulent dynamic.

Fueled by a burning desire for independence and self-expression, Starte sought an unlikely ally in Children Family Services. With unwavering determination, she seized this platform to speak her truth and demand recognition of her perspectives. Through these fearless interactions, Starte unapologetically asserted her need for autonomy and her hunger to break free from the oppressive shackles of her home.

Children Family Services became a lifeline for Starte, offering her a haven to unleash her innermost thoughts and emotions. In these sessions, she bared her soul, purging herself of the pain and frustration that had been buried deep within. The counselors listened with empathy and understanding, providing validation and guidance that gave Starte a sense of control over her tumultuous life. And as she poured out her heart, Starte's voice grew louder and more persistent, demanding to be heard and understood in her journey towards self-discovery.

With every session, Starte revealed the dark corners of her psyche, each confession a step towards healing. And amidst the chaos, Children Family Services stood as an unwavering pillar of support, empowering Starte with the tools she needed to navigate the treacherous waters of adolescence. It was through this powerful alliance that Starte found solace and strength, paving the way for her transformation into a confident young woman who refused to be silenced or confined by society's expectations.

Starte's journey was also deeply intertwined with her faith. Guided by the teachings of the Quran, she often reflected on the verses that resonated with her experiences. One such verse was:

> *"And never say of anything, 'Indeed, I will do that tomorrow,' Except [when adding], 'If Allah wills.'" (Quran 18:23-24)*

This verse encapsulated the essence of Starte's approach to life. It reminded her of the importance of humility and the acknowledgment that all plans are subject to the will of Allah. This understanding brought a sense of peace and acceptance to her journey, allowing her to navigate the uncertainties of life with a grounded perspective.

Another verse that guided her was:

> "And We have certainly honored the children of Adam and carried them on land and sea and provided for them of the good things and preferred them over much of what We have created with [definite] preference." (Quran 17:70)

This verse reinforced the inherent dignity and honor bestowed upon every human being, including Starte. It reminded her of her worth and the unique purpose she held in the world. These reflections were a source of strength and guidance, helping her navigate the complexities of her life with faith and resilience.

Her faith was a constant companion, offering solace during her darkest moments. The teachings of the Quran provided a moral compass, guiding her decisions and actions. Starte found comfort in the idea that her life was part of a larger divine plan, which helped her accept the unpredictability of her circumstances. The spiritual support she derived from her faith was instrumental in her ability to persevere and find meaning in her experiences.

Despite the tumultuous nature of her early years, Starte's academic journey was marked by remarkable achievements. From a young age, she was instilled with a love for learning by her guardians, particularly Aunt Debra. Their constant emphasis on the value of education helped Starte excel in her studies, showcasing her keen intellect and insatiable thirst for knowledge.

Her academic accomplishments were not just a testament to her intelligence and hard work but also a reflection of the unwavering support and encouragement from her family. She received numerous certificates and accolades, each one representing a milestone in her academic journey and a recognition of her achievements across various subjects.

For Starte, education was more than just a means to an end - it was a source of endless curiosity and a relentless pursuit of knowledge. The structured environment of school provided the perfect outlet for her energy and drive, allowing her to channel it into productive endeavors. But her love for learning extended far beyond the classroom walls as well. She constantly sought out new opportunities to discover and explore, always hungry for more understanding and insight into the world around her.

Proudly displayed by her family, Starte's certificates were symbols of her resilience and potential. Each one served as a reminder of how far she had come and how much further she could go. And to her guardians, they were more than just pieces of paper - they represented the promise of a bright future for their beloved ward. They celebrated her achievements wholeheartedly, reinforcing the importance of education and personal growth in shaping a person's life path.

From a young age, Starte was a curious soul, constantly seeking out new experiences and often running away from the confines of her home. Her relationship with her mother was filled with complexity as she struggled to understand and connect with the woman who brought her into this world. The involvement of Children Family Services only added to the tangled web of Starte's upbringing. However, amidst the chaos, she found solace and guidance in her faith, which became a steady guidepost along her journey toward self-discovery.

Despite the challenges she faced, Starte never wavered in her pursuit of knowledge and growth. With the support of her guardians, she excelled academically and built a strong foundation for herself. Armed with resilience and determination, she navigated through the complexities of life, using each obstacle as an opportunity to learn and evolve.

Chapter 4
She Missed the Path

The promising life of Starte Leoniece Grace Thomas was violently ripped away, consumed by the deadly grip of substance abuse at the tender age of 18. Her final moments were a heart-wrenching departure from the once vibrant and curious young woman who yearned to explore the world with an insatiable hunger. But that bright light was cruelly snuffed out, leaving behind only a trail of shattered dreams and unanswerable questions.

Starte's descent into addiction was a slow, torturous decline but ultimately unstoppable. Despite excelling academically and receiving unwavering love from her family, she battled invisible demons that ravaged her from within. The weight of adolescence, coupled with an insatiable thirst for new experiences, drove her down a treacherous road that stole her life and left her family grappling with an unfillable void.

Her days turned into nights of desperate longing for solace, but each high only pulled her deeper into a relentless abyss. She struggled silently, hiding the storm that raged within her soul, masking her pain with fleeting moments of euphoria that ultimately led her to a place of no return. The dark shadows of addiction gradually obscured the bright future that once lay before her.

And on that fateful day, her choices culminated in a fatal overdose that ravaged her body beyond repair. The news of her death sent shockwaves through her loved ones and community, shattering their hearts and leaving them grappling with an incomprehensible void. The brilliant light that was Starte had been mercilessly extinguished, leaving behind only memories and an overwhelming sense of anguish and loss.

Starte's story is a haunting reminder of the fragile nature of life and the devastating power of addiction. Her family and friends are left clinging to the remnants of her existence, haunted by what might have been. The world lost a radiant soul, a promising future, and a young woman whose potential will forever remain unrealized. Her legacy is a poignant call to action, a desperate plea to save others from the same tragic fate that befell her.

The death of Starte had a profound and lasting impact on her mother, forever altering the woman she once was. The pain of losing a child is incomprehensible, and for Starte's mother, it was compounded by the knowledge that her daughter's decisions ultimately led to her tragic demise. The game of cat-and-mouse they had played for years had ended in the most devastating way possible, leaving Starte's mother consumed by an overwhelming sense of guilt and grief.

Every moment was haunted by thoughts of "what ifs" and "if only," the constant questioning of choices made while trying to guide and protect her daughter. The constant fear and worry that had plagued her during Starte's runaway episodes were now replaced with a heart-wrenching sorrow that seemed impossible. The once lively and vibrant household now felt empty and lonely.

But the ripple effect of Starte's choices extended far beyond just her immediate family. Friends and members of the community who had watched her grow up and admired her intelligence and passion for life were also shattered by the loss of such a promising young soul. The feeling of grief was all-encompassing, touching everyone who had known her and had hoped for her bright future. Her untimely passing served as a sad reminder of the fragility of life and the far-reaching consequences our choices can have.

The story of Starte, though marred with tragedy, offers a poignant reflection on the gravity of our choices in life. It serves as a stark reminder of the importance of being conscious and receiving support when navigating through the tumultuous journey of adolescence and young adulthood. Starte's life was marked by both brilliance and struggle, making her a testament to the power of our decisions and the paths we choose to follow.

Star had never been a drug user. Her death certificate showed no signs of narcotics, only fentanyl and an unknown substance. We suspect that someone laced her sinus medication with the deadly drug.

This contemplation urges us to have a deeper understanding of the immense felonies faced by young people and the critical need for falling prey to such nuances. It also highlights the crucial role played by family, community, and social services in guiding and nurturing young individuals through their formative years.

The tragic end of Starte's journey serves as a potent reminder for us to be vigilant and compassionate when addressing issues related to substance abuse and mental health. It calls for proactive measures to educate and empower youth to make informed choices that pave the way for a brighter and healthier future. Her story is an enduring testament to the dire consequences of neglecting these pivotal aspects of youth development.

The Quran, a sacred text that serves as a source of guidance and comfort for millions around the world, offers solace in times of distress and reflection. In Starte's story, there is one verse that echoes with a deep resonance:

> *"And whoever does evil or wrongs himself but then seeks forgiveness of Allah will find Allah Forgiving and Merciful." (Quran 4:110)*

These words speak to the boundless compassion and mercy of Allah, providing hope even in the depths of our most grievous mistakes. They serve as a reminder that no matter how far we may stray, the door to redemption and forgiveness is always open. This powerful message holds particular significance for those reflecting on Starte's life and the choices she made.

For her mother and loved ones, this verse brings a measure of comfort. It reassures them that despite the tragic end to Starte's journey, there is always the possibility of divine mercy and forgiveness. It encourages them to find solace in their faith and to take comfort in the belief that Starte now rests in the care of a merciful and forgiving Creator.

This reflection also serves as a poignant reminder for the living. It calls upon us to seek forgiveness for our transgressions and to strive towards making better choices in our lives. It highlights the importance of showing compassion, understanding, and support for those battling their struggles, reminding us that we are all in need of mercy and forgiveness.

The tragic events surrounding Starte's overdose and untimely death serve as a sobering reminder of the consequences of our choices and the profound impact they can have on our lives and the lives of those we love. As her final breaths escaped her and her body grew cold, the weight of regret and sorrow settled deeply into the hearts of all who knew and loved her.

Starte's story is a testament to the complexities of adolescence, a tumultuous time filled with uncertainties and pressures that can lead to dangerous decisions. Her untimely death serves as a poignant reminder of the critical importance of support and guidance for young people. It highlights the dire consequences that can arise from neglect or lack of understanding.

As her mother grapples with overwhelming pain, the community mourns alongside her, united in grief. In this shared sorrow, there is a deep reflection on the value of life and the fragility of it all. The Quranic verse offers a glimmer of hope, a reminder that forgiveness and mercy are always within reach, even in the darkest of times.

Through Starte's story, we are reminded of our responsibility to nurture and guide our youth, to provide them with the tools and understanding they need to navigate their challenges. We must create an environment where they feel supported and empowered to make healthy and positive choices. Though her life was cut short, Starte's legacy lives on, serving as a guiding light toward a more compassionate and supportive world for all youth.

Chapter 5
A Light Gone Too Soon

The decision to run away from home was a tumultuous one for Starte Leoniece Grace Thomas. She longed to break free from the turmoil and constraints of her family life, but leaving behind everything she knew and loved was daunting. As she set out on her journey, mixed emotions flooded her mind - the exhilaration of newfound freedom clashing with the fear of an uncertain future.

Despite her determination to find peace in her new life, Starte quickly learned that being a runaway was far from romantic. The streets were harsh and unforgiving, each day bringing a new set of challenges. Hunger gnawed at her stomach, cold seeped into her bones, and danger loomed around every corner. Trust was a rarity, and self-preservation became her top priority. With every encounter, she emerged more broken and lonely than before, yet still held onto a glimmer of hope for a brighter tomorrow.

However, as time passed and her struggles intensified, Starte's resolve began to wane. She clung desperately to the belief that things would improve, but desperation clouded her judgment and led her to make choices she never thought possible. The dream of reclaiming her life seemed further out of reach with each passing day, and Starte couldn't help but wonder if it had all been worth it.

In reflecting on Starte's journey, the harrowing truth of the necessity to share one's pain and seek help from trusted individuals becomes painfully evident. Starte's silence, coupled with her futile attempt to shoulder her burdens alone, did nothing but magnify her suffering, plunging her deeper into the abyss of despair. Her story is a poignant reminder that reaching out for support is not a sign of weakness but rather a courageous and essential step toward healing.

Opening up about one's struggles to family, friends, or a trusted mentor is an act of bravery that can provide immeasurable relief and guidance. These individuals can offer a different perspective, practical assistance, and the emotional support needed to counter the overwhelming sense of isolation and hopelessness. The weight of one's troubles is halved when shared, and the act of confiding in others can lead to breakthroughs that might seem unattainable when struggling alone.

Communities and relationships are the bedrock of human experience, built on mutual care and understanding. Leaning on these pillars in times of need can be the lifeline that prevents one from sinking into the depths of despair. A heartfelt conversation, a comforting presence, or simply knowing that someone cares can make an astonishing difference. In the midst of suffering, recognizing the strength in vulnerability and the power of connection can transform the path to recovery.

Personal joy is a beacon of hope and a fundamental aspect of a fulfilling life. For Starte, the pursuit of joy was marred by her circumstances, casting a shadow over her path and obscuring the light of happiness. Yet, it remains essential for everyone to seek out what genuinely brings them happiness. Joy is not merely a fleeting emotion but a profound state of being that nourishes the soul and enriches life. Engaging in activities that uplift the spirit, spending time with loved ones, and nurturing one's passions can provide a sense of purpose and direction. These pursuits create moments of respite from life's hardships, allowing one to reconnect with the essence of what makes life beautiful.

Finding joy often involves embracing simple pleasures—walking in nature, enjoying a hobby, or sharing laughter with friends. These experiences, though seemingly small, accumulate to form a robust foundation of happiness. They remind us that even amidst the turmoil, there are pockets of peace and delight to be found. Moreover, nurturing one's passions—whether it be art, music, reading, or any other interest—can be particularly empowering. These passions serve as a sanctuary, offering solace and a sense of accomplishment that fortifies the spirit against adversity.

Equally important to the pursuit of joy is the conscious effort to avoid dangerous situations. The allure of certain experiences, particularly those involving unethical behaviors, often masks the peril they bring. These situations can seduce with promises of escape or excitement, yet they conceal the devastating consequences that follow. The immediate gratification they offer is fleeting, leaving behind a trail of physical harm and moral erosion. Engaging in such behaviors, or wrong people, not only jeopardizes one's health but also erodes the moral and emotional fabric of an individual, leading to a spiral of degradation and regret.

It is crucial to develop the discernment to recognize and steer clear of environments and individuals that pose a risk to one's well-being. This discernment is an act of self-respect and self-preservation, safeguarding one's journey toward a fulfilling life. By choosing paths that align with one's values and well-being, individuals can build a life that is not only joyful but also sustainable and true to their authentic selves.

In the context of seeking joy and safety, the Quran offers profound wisdom. As it is written,

> *"O you who have believed, seek help through patience and prayer. Indeed, Allah is with the patient." (Quran 2:153).*

This verse serves as a powerful reminder to find strength and guidance through patience and prayer, grounding oneself in faith during turbulent times. Patience, in this context, is not mere passive endurance but an active, steadfast commitment to maintaining hope and integrity even when faced with challenges.

Another verse that resonates deeply is,

> *"And whoever fears Allah - He will make for him a way out and will provide for him from where he does not expect. And whoever relies upon Allah - then He is sufficient for him" (Quran 65:2-3).*

This verse underscores the importance of trust and reliance on divine wisdom. It reassures believers that, even in dire circumstances, there is a path laid out by Allah that leads to relief and unexpected blessings. This divine assurance fosters a sense of security and optimism, encouraging individuals to hold on to their faith.

Moreover, the verse

> *"So be patient. Indeed, the promise of Allah is truth. And ask forgiveness for your sin and exalt [Allah] with praise of your Lord in the evening and the morning" (Quran 40:55)*

highlights the importance of patience and constant devotion. It reminds believers that Allah's promises are unwavering and that maintaining a routine of praise and seeking forgiveness strengthens one's spiritual resilience.

Embracing these verses, one can find the resilience to navigate life's challenges and the clarity to pursue genuine joy, securely anchored in faith and self-awareness. The strength drawn from patience and prayer equips individuals to face adversity with courage and to seek joy with a steadfast heart. It is through this balance of seeking happiness and avoiding harm, guided by faith and wisdom, that one can achieve a truly fulfilling and enriched life.

Tragically, Starte's life was cut short due to her presence in the wrong place at the wrong time. Everything was wrong! In her desperate quest for belonging and relief from her inner pain, she found herself entangled with people who led her further astray. These associations indulged her into the abyss of substance abuse, ultimately leading to her untimely demise. Her story is a heart-wrenching testament to how the search for solace can tragically backfire when one falls into the wrong company.

Her passing is a stark reminder of the destructive influence that negative associations can have on one's life. It underscores the importance of choosing companions who embody righteousness and holiness, as emphasized in the Quran:

> *"And cooperate in righteousness and piety, but do not cooperate in sin and aggression." (Quran 5:2).*

This verse serves as a divine caution to seek and foster relationships that encourage good deeds and moral integrity.

The impact of one's social circle on their choices and behavior cannot be overstated. Positive influences can uplift, guide, and provide the support necessary to overcome life's challenges. Conversely, negative influences can derail even the strongest of individuals, leading them down a path of self-destruction. Starte's tragic end is a poignant illustration of this truth, highlighting the critical need for discernment in choosing one's companions.

The Quran further advises on the importance of surrounding oneself with good influences:

> *"O you who have believed, fear Allah and be with those who are true." (Quran 9:119).*

This verse emphasizes the value of honesty and integrity, suggesting that being in the company of truthful and righteous individuals can help one stay on the right path. Such associations are not just beneficial but essential for spiritual and moral well-being.

Moreover, the verse

> *"And remind, for indeed, the reminder benefits the believers." (Quran 51:55)*

speaks to the importance of continuous mutual encouragement among believers. Regular reminders and support from a righteous community can reinforce one's resolve to live a life aligned with moral and ethical principles.

In essence, Starte's story is a solemn reminder of the profound impact our companions have on our lives. It underscores the need to seek out and maintain relationships that are rooted in righteousness and holiness. By doing so, we not only protect ourselves from the pitfalls of negative influences but also create a support system that fosters growth, healing, and genuine happiness. The wisdom of the Quran guides us to be mindful of our associations, urging us to choose those who uplift and steer us toward a life of virtue and purpose.

Chapter 6
Deceit

As the sun dipped below the horizon, casting a warm glow over the familiar city, a sense of anticipation filled the air. It had been weeks since I had laid eyes on Star. Weeks since the news of Stars running away spread throughout the community of loved ones and peers. It caused so much worry and concern for me and those who cared deeply for my missing child.

But tonight was different hope was circulating among our loved ones. The tree surrounding my backyard stood tall and proud, its branches reaching out like welcoming arms.

And then, as if summoned by the collective yearning of those who awaited, there was rustling in the distance. From the shadows making their way toward the house, it was Star as she drew closer. The tension I felt in the air gave way to a wave of relief and joy. Tears flowed freely as stories were shared and laughter rang out. Starte was home for a brief moment, I had given her 600 hundred dollars through the cash app, and she came home. Safe from the noisy streets of Chicago, she was here with her siblings and a family who loved her. However, it would not be long before she would become deceived by the predator, who she thought was her boyfriend. More than 20 years her senior. Believed to be a trafficker of women. A female sex solicitor.

And just like shadows of betrayal, Star had been lured away again into a web of deceit. Her trust shattered, and her heart was heavy with the weight of his betrayal. She had believed in the promises whispered by false friends only to find herself trapped in a tangled mess of lies and manipulation. He was not the music producer she envisioned. He was a trafficker of women who used her to try and lure other young women into this web of deceit.

As Star wandered through unfamiliar streets, the echoes of false assurances haunted her thoughts, casting dark shadows upon her path. Every corner turned, every face encountered seemed to mock her misplaced trust, leaving her adrift in a sea of uncertainty and disillusionment. The woman she called her mom in the streets knew her predator and hid the predatory relationship, filling her head with the belief she loved her while calling my phone complaining that my young teenage daughter was trying to seduce the young men she frequented. The woman who went to work the day I buried Star and never brought her a flower, the woman who housed my under aged daughter at times then turned her back on her for being young and beautiful.

As Star began to discover so much deceit in her last days, she began to want out. To travel a different path, but time was running out for my dear daughter. Alone and adrift, Star struggled to make sense of the deception that had led her astray. The once familiar world now seemed alien and hostile. Every smile is a potential snare every kind gesture a veiled threat.

As the days passed, the weight of betrayal bore down upon her, threatening to crush her spirit and extinguish the flicker of hope that still burned within her. But deep down beneath the layers of her hurt and anger, a seed of resilience began to take root, nourished by the realization that she was not alone in her suffering.

Slowly and tentatively, Star reached out to her aunt, my sister, who offered her solace and support. She was hesitant to trust again but unwilling to let the shadows of betrayal consume her entirely. To Stars' surprise, she had true friends and family who stood ready to offer a hand to guide her out of the darkness and into the light of understanding and forgiveness.

Through her healing power of genuine connections and wisdom gained from her ordeal, Star began to piece together the fragments of her shattered trust weaving her into a tapestry of resilience and newfound strength. She took to her Facebook page and expressed disappointment in her current situation and the need to escape it. But by this time, her untimely overdose stole her life. No other drugs were found in her system, just fentanyl and promethazine. We wondered how it got into her system. We will never know. Just know that the gentleman in question sent me his phone number, trying to explain her untimely death and offered me to come pick up her cell phone and belongings. As I traveled that highway in so much disbelief, I could only imagine what I would discover or how I would react when I saw this predator that I had been unaware of. Street connects, and old comrades and Muslim brothers went with me almost 15 or 20 deep. As we were led inside to the area in the house where my baby died, her fluids were still there, wet and cold. I fell to my knees to touch what remained of my baby's last fluids.

I could not bear to keep holding a conversation with this predator. As I motioned for everyone to leave, he kept trying to explain his recollection of the events that stole Star's life, but his explanations kept falling on deaf ears. We saw the rooms where outside locks had been removed to stage that crime scene. We saw other young women's clothing there. We were so confused that the detectives appeared not to put two and two together. After my visit to the police station and questioning what they knew with what we discovered it appeared something had changed. What I will never know. As I prepared myself to bury Star and fight the transgression she had endured, a call came across the phone and said the predator had crashed his car, and it burst into flames. He died the day I laid my precious Starte to rest. I am so convinced this was a huge sex trafficking organization. I will never know because there appear to be no more perpetrators. A man with 22 warrants out for his arrest was allowed to continue this type of behavior.

My daughter knew that while the scars of deception lingered, she was emerging from the crucible of betrayal transformed. She just never got another chance to Think before She Ran.

Chapter 7
Footprints in the sand

Each footprint is a testament to my inner turmoil, etched by the relentless tides of life. Though my mortal body may lay in this earthly realm, my spirit roams wild and untamed, unchained from all worldly pain.

In the dance of the wind and sea, I am swept away by a fleeting sense of liberty. Even in death, my soul takes flight, guided by the warm embrace of Allah's eternal light. With each step I take along the shoreline, the soft sand shifts beneath my feet like a comforting embrace from the ocean.

As the sun dips below the horizon, casting a golden glow over the tranquil beach, I walk with a purpose, leaving behind a trail of delicate footprints that glisten in the fading light. These imprints, however, were not made by the living but by Starte - a young Muslim girl who departed this world too soon. She was known for her kind heart and free spirit, always trusting others even when it may have been dangerous to do so.

As the waves gently lap at the shore, erasing the imprints of the day, Starte's footprints remain untouched as if preserved by an unseen hand. Those who pass by can't help but feel a sense of peace and serenity in the presence of these ghostly marks in the sand.

As the sun set and darkness blanketed the beach, the ghostly footprints of Starte, a Muslim girl taken too soon, burned with an eerie glow. Her soul beckoned to all who passed by, a warning and a plea for remembrance.

Remember me, she whispered in the wind, as you run from your troubles. But be cautious, for the path ahead may be treacherous and full of unseen dangers. In death, I have learned that running away brings only temporary relief, while facing our fears head-on can bring true healing and growth.

Closing Thoughts

As we reach the end of this journey, it is crucial to reflect on the lessons learned and the stark realities faced by runaways like Star. The world is full of dangers, and the predators who seek to exploit the vulnerable come in many forms. Awareness and caution can be lifesaving.

Predators come in all forms.

1. Online Predators

In today's digital age, online predators use social media, chat rooms, online gaming platforms, and other online spaces to target and groom vulnerable individuals. Star met Tone online, posing as a record producer. After Star's death, I discovered how he connected with young women through his page, pretending to be a music producer. It is essential to be cautious about sharing personal information online and to avoid meeting up with someone you've only met online without proper precautions. Star believed Tone was going to make her famous because his site showcased music he allegedly produced. This illusion cost her dearly.

2. Human Traffickers

Human traffickers often target vulnerable individuals, including runaways like Star, for exploitation. They use manipulation, coercion, and force to control their victims. Runaways must be cautious about accepting offers of help or promises that seem too good to be true. These predators are skilled at spotting desperation and exploiting it for their own gain.

3. Sexual Predators

Sexual predators may target runaways for grooming, sexual exploitation, or abuse. They often establish inappropriate relationships and make their victims feel uncomfortable. Runaways should be wary of adults who display excessive interest or attempt to isolate them from their support networks. Trusting one's instincts is crucial in these situations.

4. Drug Dealers and Gangs

Runaways are at risk of being recruited by drug dealers or gangs who exploit them for criminal activities. Involvement in illegal activities can quickly spiral into a dangerous cycle of exploitation and violence. Runaways need to avoid such entanglements and seek help from authorities if they feel threatened or pressured.

5. Posing as Caregivers

Some predators pose as caring individuals, offering shelter, support, or assistance to runaways, only to exploit them later. Runaways should be cautious about accepting help from strangers and verify the credibility of any organization or individual offering assistance. Trust must be earned, not given freely.

6. Romantic Manipulators:

Traffickers may pose as romantic partners to gain the trust of runaways before exploiting them. This was Star's case; she believed Tone loved her. Runaways should be cautious about entering into romantic relationships with individuals they do not know well or who make them uncomfortable. Trusting too quickly can lead to devastating consequences.

Runaways must be aware of these risks, trust their instincts, and seek help from trusted adults, authorities, or organizations specializing in helping runaway youth. Education, awareness, and access to support services are key to protecting oneself from predators. The lessons learned from Star's tragic story serve as a poignant reminder of the importance of vigilance and the dire consequences of misplaced trust.

Through understanding these dangers, we can honor Star's memory by striving to protect other vulnerable individuals from similar fates. Let us commit to creating a world where every child and teenager feels safe, supported, and valued.

In the wake of her daughter's tragic passing, Starte's mother found herself at a crossroads, her life irrevocably altered by the searing pain of loss. Overwhelmed by grief and desperately searching for solace, she embarked on a journey of faith that would profoundly transform her life. Her introduction to Islam came through a close friend who offered her a compassionate ear and spiritual guidance during her darkest days, providing a glimmer of hope when she felt most lost.

Initially, she approached Islam with hesitation, her heart and mind weighed down by sorrow. However, as she began to explore the teachings of Islam, she found a deep sense of comfort in its messages of patience, resilience, and hope. The Quran became a sanctuary for her weary soul, its verses like balm to her wounds, offering her a sense of peace and understanding amidst the chaos of her emotions. Each passage she read resonated with her, speaking to the universal truths of human suffering and the promise of divine mercy and justice.

As she delved deeper into her studies, she discovered the principles of faith that resonated profoundly with her own experiences of loss and longing. The Islamic teachings on the temporality of life, the importance of enduring hardship with grace, and the ultimate reunion with loved ones in the hereafter provided her with a new perspective on her grief. She began to see her pain as part of a larger, divine plan, and this realization brought her a measure of acceptance and tranquility.

Embracing Islam provided her with a renewed outlook on life and death. The belief in Allah's greater plan and the hope of reuniting with Starte in the afterlife became beacons of light in her journey through grief. This hope was not just a distant, abstract idea but a tangible source of strength that helped her endure the daily heartache of living without her daughter. The rituals of prayer and the practice of patience became her anchors, grounding her in moments of overwhelming sadness.

Moreover, the community she found within her new faith offered her unwavering support and a sense of belonging. She was welcomed with open arms by fellow believers who understood her pain and offered her their empathy and encouragement. This new family, bound by faith, helped her navigate the turbulent emotions that accompanied her loss. They prayed with her, shared their own stories of hardship and endurance, and reminded her that she was not alone in her suffering.

Through her exploration of Islam, Starte's mother found not only solace but also a purpose. She became an active member of her faith community, participating in charitable activities and offering support to others who were experiencing their trials. Her journey of faith, born out of immense sorrow, transformed into a journey of healing and giving. She drew strength from the Quran and the teachings of the Prophet Muhammad, and in turn, she became a source of strength for others.

In the end, Starte's mother's journey through grief and faith is a testament to the transformative power of spiritual discovery. Islam provided her with the tools to cope with her loss, the community to support her, and the hope to sustain her. It allowed her to honor her daughter's memory in a way that brought her peace and purpose, turning her profound tragedy into a catalyst for personal and communal growth. Through faith, she found a way to carry on, her heart forever linked to her daughters by the threads of love and hope.

Despite the solace she found in her faith, Starte's mother's heartache remained a constant companion, an ever-present shadow that followed her through each day. The pain of losing her daughter was a wound that refused to heal, no matter how much time passed. She often found herself revisiting memories of Starte, her mind flooded with images of her daughter's bright smile, her infectious laughter, and her insatiable curiosity about the world. These memories, while cherished, also served as poignant reminders of the life that was so cruelly cut short.

Each day brought new moments of reflection and longing. The sight of children playing in the park, the sound of laughter echoing through the hallways, and the milestones that other parents celebrated with their children all served as painful reminders of what could have been. Every graduation, every birthday, and every small achievement of other children magnified the void left by Starte's absence. Her mother's dreams for her daughter—dreams of seeing her grow, succeed, and find her happiness—were now unfulfilled promises, haunting echoes of a future that would never come to pass.

The depth of her grief was immeasurable, a sorrow so profound that it permeated every aspect of her life. Her tears were a testament to the profound love she held for Starte, a love that was as deep and enduring as her grief. Yet, in her longing and heartache, she found a way to honor her daughter's memory in a meaningful way. She channeled her pain into action, determined to ensure that Starte's story would serve as a warning and a source of hope for others.

By sharing her story, Starte's mother hoped to shine a light on the dangers of addiction and the importance of seeking help. She spoke openly about the struggles her daughter faced, the signs she had missed, and the devastating consequences of substance abuse. She aimed to educate other parents, to help them recognize the warning signs, and to encourage them to take action before it was too late. She wanted to break the stigma surrounding addiction and mental health, fostering a culture of understanding and support.

Her advocacy efforts were not limited to speaking engagements and community events. She also became involved in various support groups and organizations dedicated to helping families affected by addiction. Through these channels, she offered her support to other grieving parents, shared resources, and worked to raise awareness about the importance of mental health care. Her involvement provided her with a sense of purpose, a way to transform her tragedy into a beacon of hope for others.

In doing so, her grief became a driving force for advocacy and awareness. She found strength in knowing that her efforts could prevent other families from experiencing the same heartache. Her pain, while ever-present, was given a new direction, one that brought a sense of healing and fulfillment. By turning her sorrow into a mission of compassion and education, she honored Starte's memory in the most profound way possible—by helping others and making a difference in their lives.

Through her advocacy, Starte's mother not only preserved her daughter's legacy but also created a ripple effect of change and awareness. Her story resonated with many, touching hearts and inspiring action. It was a testament to the enduring power of love and the strength of the human spirit. Even in the face of unimaginable loss, she found a way to rise, to fight, and to ensure that Starte's light continued to shine, illuminating the path for others to follow.

Throughout this arduous journey, the support of friends, family, and her newfound faith community proved to be invaluable pillars of strength. They stood by her side, unwavering in their commitment to offer compassion and understanding, even in the darkest of moments. Their presence became a source of solace, providing her with the courage to face each day and the determination to keep moving forward, no matter how heavy the burden of grief weighed upon her shoulders.

In addition to the steadfast support of those closest to her, Starte's mother was also touched by the kindness of strangers and acquaintances alike. Their heartfelt condolences and gestures of sympathy created a network of care that enveloped her in love during her time of need. Each comforting word, each shared prayer, and each silent hug became a lifeline in her sea of grief, offering a glimmer of hope amidst the overwhelming darkness.

But the support she received extended far beyond emotional comfort. Her community rallied around her, offering practical assistance with daily tasks, financial support, and, perhaps most importantly, their willingness to listen simply. Their collective effort served as a constant reminder that she was not alone in her pain, that her daughter's story had touched the lives of many, and that together, they could find a way to navigate the treacherous waters of grief and healing.

The outpouring of love and support from friends, family, and even strangers served as a beacon of hope in the midst of despair, a reminder that even in the darkest of times, there are always rays of light to guide the way. Their unwavering presence and selfless acts of kindness became the cornerstone of Starte's mother's journey through grief, providing her with the strength and resilience to continue her path toward healing.

In the end, it was the collective efforts of her community that helped her find solace in the midst of sorrow and hope in the face of despair. Their love and support became the threads that wove together the fabric of her healing, binding her heart to theirs in a shared journey of loss, remembrance, and, ultimately, resilience.

The final chapter of Starte's mother's story resonates with the heartfelt words of those who knew and cherished Starte deeply. Her friends recall her as a vibrant soul overflowing with life and untapped potential. They reminisce about her acts of kindness, the infectious laughter that filled the room whenever she was around, and the dreams she harbored for her future. These memories serve as poignant reminders of the radiant light that Starte brought into their lives—a light that continues to shine brightly, undiminished by her physical absence.

As family members share their reflections, the depth of their sorrow and the profound void left by Starte's passing becomes palpable. They recount the precious moments of her childhood, the milestones she reached, and the unique bond she shared with each of them. Their words convey not only the magnitude of their loss but also their unwavering commitment to preserving Starte's memory, ensuring that she remains forever enshrined in their hearts and minds.

Loved ones from Starte's faith community offer poignant reflections on the impact of her story. They speak of the profound lessons gleaned from her life—the importance of resilience in the face of adversity, the enduring power of love, and the transformative nature of faith. Starte's mother, in her journey of grief and faith, becomes a source of inspiration for all who hear her story. Her unwavering strength and resilience serve as a beacon of hope in the darkest of times, reminding others of the comfort and solace that can be found in unwavering faith.

As we bring this journey to a close, we reflect on the life of Starte Leoniece Grace Thomas and the indelible mark she left on all who knew her. Her story is one of promise and potential cut tragically short, but it is also a story of love, resilience, and hope. Through the lens of her mother's journey of faith, we witness the transformative power of belief and the strength that comes from a supportive community.

Though Starte may no longer be with us in the physical sense, her legacy lives on—in the hearts of those who loved her, in the advocacy efforts her story has inspired, and in the invaluable lessons learned from her life. Her memory serves as a poignant reminder to cherish our loved ones, to seek help in times of need, and to offer unwavering support to one another through life's darkest moments. Though Starte's physical light may have been extinguished too soon, her spirit endures, guiding us toward a future where no light is ever extinguished before its time.

If Tears Could Build A Stairway

If tears could build a stairway
And memories were a lane
We would walk right up to Heaven
And bring you back again

No farewell words were spoken
No time to say goodbye
You were gone before we knew it
And only God knows why

Our hearts still ache in sadness
And secret tears still flow
What it meant to lose you
No one will ever know

But know we know you want us
To mourn for you no more
To remember all the happy times
Life still has much in store

Since you'll never be forgotten
We pledge to you today
A hallowed place within our hearts
Is where you'll always stay

www.ingramcontent.com/pod-product-compliance
Lightning Source LLC
LaVergne TN
LVHW051040070526
838201LV00066B/4868